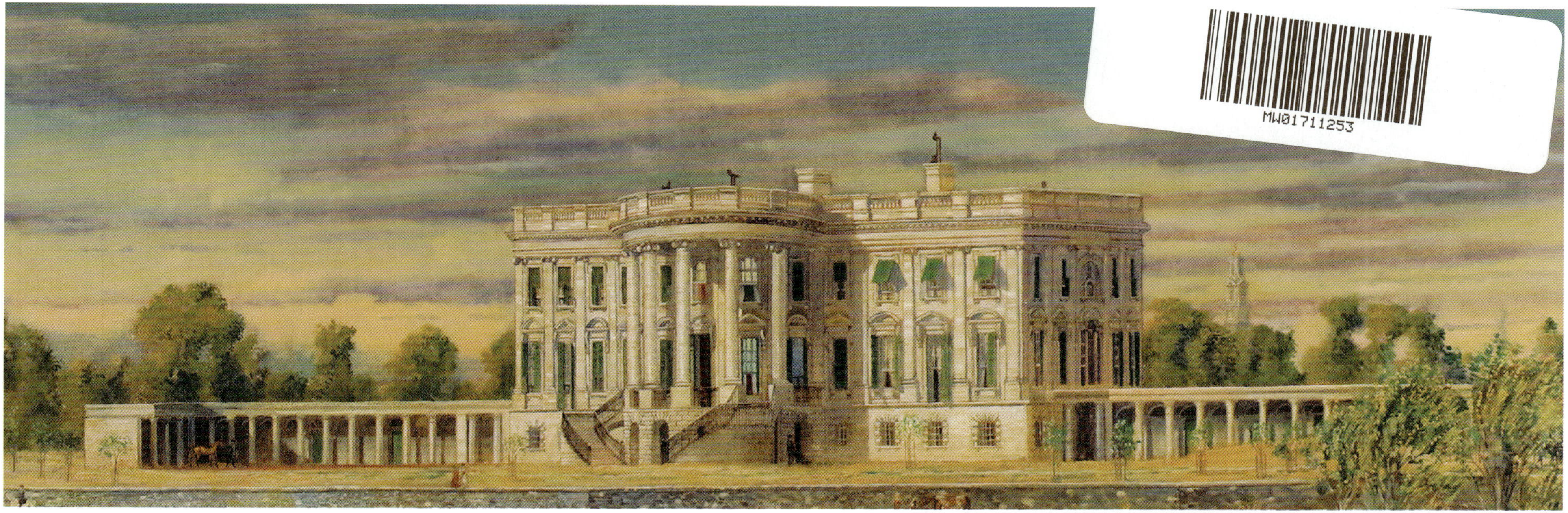

An Artist Visits The White House Past

Paintings by Peter Waddell

Text by William Seale

Commissioned by The White House Historical Association

THE **WHITE HOUSE**
HISTORICAL ASSOCIATION
50TH ANNIVERSARY

The White House Historical Association is a nonprofit organization, chartered on November 3, 1961, to enhance understanding, appreciation, and enjoyment of the historic White House. Income from the sale of the association's books and guides is returned to the publications program and is used as well to acquire historical furnishings and memorabilia for the White House.

Address inquiries to:
White House Historical Association
740 Jackson Place, N.W., Washington, D.C. 20006
www.whitehousehistory.org

For more information about the paintings in this exhibit visit http://www.whitehousehistory.org/history/waddell

ISBN 978-1-931917-15-5

Printed in the USA

Introduction

THE FOURTEEN PAINTINGS IN THIS EXHIBITION WERE COMMISSIONED FROM PETER WADDELL BEGINNING IN 2004 BY THE WHITE HOUSE HISTORICAL ASSOCIATION. It was the association's wish that the artist create well-researched pictures representing different periods from the White House past that were not drawn, painted, or photographed definitively in their own times.

Rather than attempting to capture great events, Waddell decided to take odd moments in presidential life at the White House. Thus you will see Dolley Madison entertaining in her drawing room; the second President Adams taking a dangerous swim; a social worker's visit with a relaxed Abraham Lincoln in his office; a great cheese placed in the center of Andrew Jackson's East Room; Theodore Roosevelt's son and pets in the now-vanished conservatory, and other interludes, not least one bright and lively representation of the Entrance Hall showing the Tiffany glass screen, gone now for over a hundred years.

Re-creating the past is nothing new to art, and representing domestic scenes was well known in the seventeenth and eighteenth centuries. As with movies yet to come, the scenes themselves were usually secondary to the people portrayed in them. Peter Waddell's White House pictures relate more to nineteenth-century traditions, when houses and interiors were painted for their own sake. Private living quarters, notably in the palaces of Eastern Europe—Austria for example—were often preserved in oil or watercolor, for all but the basic furnishings were in place for only a season at court and removed elsewhere when that was over.

The conscious attempt to illustrate historic interiors as interiors, with costumed figures in them was a different matter entirely and saw its first significant early expression in *The Mansions of England in the Olden Time*, a large folio published in 1840 by the lithographer Joseph Nash. An antiquarian and genre artist, Nash challenged the eighteenth-century idea that early houses in England had been cold and uncomfortable. His plates celebrated their human and picturesque qualities. The galleries, bedchambers and halls of England's most notable historic houses were rendered by Nash in detail, as they might have been in the times of the Tudors and Stuarts. To his old houses he added costumed characters, anonymous, most of them, in the course of everyday life.

How Nash's scenes differed from most others was that his represented the antithesis of the decorated room setting that was well established by 1840. The concept of creating interiors as ensembles of unified design had come into its own in the early nineteenth century, and for many years inspired a whole genre of paintings for the market of fashion it represented. Decorated rooms boasted the owner's good taste, although that was subject to judgment. Use of the medium of paint and canvas for house illustrations died out when photography took over. In Nash's lithographed rooms the architecture and characters were the main features, furniture and other objects being secondary and always sparse.

Peter Waddell's White House paintings represent a combination of both approaches. They are antiquarian, to be sure, in their scholarship. The architecture is rendered as it exists or, in some cases "restored" to the way some vanished or altered piece is known to have looked. Accurate details of furniture and costume are brought in not for style, but to enrich the representation of human use, for it is the human side of presidents that interests us most in visiting the White House. The scenes are believable, and in painting them Waddell has wished to entertain as well as inform.

The late Professor Mario Praz, scholar of interiors, liked this comment about interiors by the German philosopher Walter Benjamin: "The interior represents the universe for the private individual. He collects there whatever is distant, whatever is of the past. His living room is a box in the theater of the world." One pauses over this when considering the White House, where the occupants make their box seat but own neither it nor what is contained in it.

They live with what they may have acquired with public funds or what they borrow from the presidential past. They gather the chairs and tables, the portraits and tableware of their predecessors into settings for themselves during their own short tenures. A storage warehouse kept off-site is available to help with any readjustments, its contents being former White House furnishings, which by law must be retained. Every object that is returned to service carries a history of its own and has acquired another layer by the time it returns to the warehouse.

In a sense the White House is an unusual sort of family home, with a big attic. The building stands, rebuilt, remodeled, strengthened, and vigilantly maintained yet still clearly recognizable as the structure George Washington approved more than 200 years ago. Presidents come and go, arranging things as they see fit, within the context largely of what is there. The White House welcomes the new presidents with formats and procedures already well-honed over time to serve him well.

Peter Waddell's decision to venture into the past committed him to much more than pursuit of his skill with paint, brushes, and canvas. To find details he read extensively the history surrounding the fourteen episodes in his pictures. In the National Archives, Record Group 42, thousands upon thousands of pages carry one back two centuries through the intimate life of the White House and its presidents, the furniture they used, the dishes they ate upon, the services for which they had to summon tradesmen, whose faded invoices are revealing.

He studied inventories of the house, and they exist for every administration. As any government official knows, scandal-seekers fix more readily upon spending public funds for a $750 office table, which can be quickly envisioned, than a $30,000,000 highway, which is not only cumbersome to describe but rather an abstraction. At the White House great care has always been taken to keep an updated record of the government-owned contents of the building, which may vary from a gilded mirror to a kitchen pot, all potential symbols of official extravagance. When Waddell shows, for example, Andrew Jackson's East Room, he may have no precise documentation for how the Great Cheese consumed there looked, but he has pretty solid information on everything else, even the *papier-mache* stars and rays over the door that crowned Old Hickory's dramatic entrances.

Maps, letters, memoirs, and published accounts are central to any research on the White House. John Quincy Adams, in his diary written that night, literally set down guidelines for Waddell's depiction of the president's near-drowning. In his search for information, the artist consulted the visual materials. For example, for the Roosevelt conservatory he used thick files of photographs in the Prints and Photographs Division of the Library of Congress showing the long-vanished buildings; but the photographs were supplemented with the gardener's listings of tropical plants that grew beneath the glass ceilings, and the plants form the major feature of the picture.

Attempting total recall of the past is risky, no matter the medium. The easiest way to re-create the past is with the written word, for with the right words one can build mental images from sparse materials—the tall, brown autumn grass in the meadow (when you know tall brown grass was certainly present at a given place in November), or an orderly row of gilded chairs (when you know the ballroom had gilded chairs, almost certainly set in lines, given their great number).

A historical painting, however, requires more than a draftsman's ability to replicate what he finds in research. The painter is imposing his imagination upon that of the viewer. This requires skill as an artist to reach a believable, comprehensive image with which a viewer is willing to replace his own mental image of how it was. A painter achieves this in the status he gives to forms on the canvas, his interpretation of documented color alongside created color, but most of all, in the way he wakens our emotions with his use of light. Peter Waddell's White House pictures are thus his, as much as they are factual images gleaned from the documentation he has brought to them.

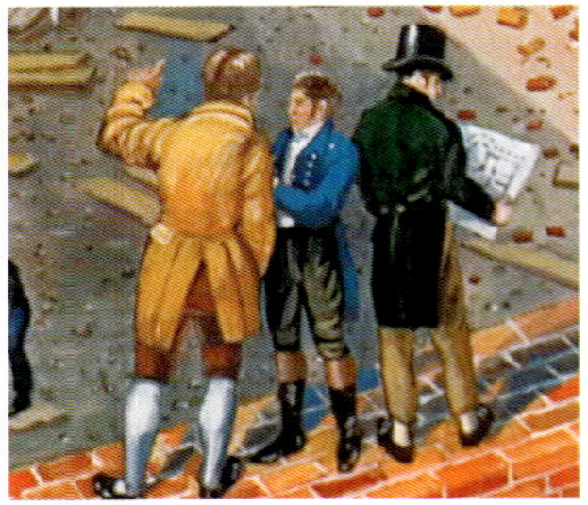

A Vision Takes Form

The White House Under Construction • 1796

AT THIS STAGE IN THE CONSTRUCTION OF THE WHITE HOUSE, 1796, the walls are rising above the second floor level. They are half way to completion. People were now beginning to see how extensive the house was to be, and they must have looked on in wonder. Larger than a statehouse and taller than most church steeples, it would have loomed above any American town of its time.

The perspective Waddell has selected is not entirely imaginary. Although it takes our eyes higher than the trees, which provided the tallest prospects around, it approximates carefully what we might have seen from a hot air balloon, that fanciful contraption introduced to Europe less than a decade before. From this useful position we see the entire construction of the White House in process. The artist has reviewed the original building receipts and contracts of the architect James Hoban (to whom President Washington entrusted the design and construction), the brick-mason Jeremiah Kale, and the stonemason Collen Williamson. None of the three, nor most builders on the job, were born in America.

From where we view the structure, the succession of rooms begins with the largest, the East Room, beneath your feet, across the parlors, Green and Red, climaxed by the oval Blue Room between them, and on to the State Dining Room. The big space with the crane in the center is the Entrance Hall. When the house was completed, not a single brick would show.

The character of construction was not different from that common in the monumental buildings in Europe two centuries before it, be they cathedrals, private houses, palaces, or civic structures. Stone was the most precious and admired of all building materials. Being costly to quarry, transport, and dress, it was used sparingly, thus, as the painting shows, the White House had outer walls of stone, backed with thick layers of cheaper soft brick. Protected from the weather, the brick stabilized the stone walls and, molded on the site, trimmed costs dramatically. The painting shows how construction at that time was self-supporting, stone laid upon stone, brick upon brick, timber pinned to timber with pegs. Except for the stone walls, this would be replaced when the contents of the historic stone shell were replaced with modern materials 150 years later, when the White House was rebuilt in structural steel and concrete.

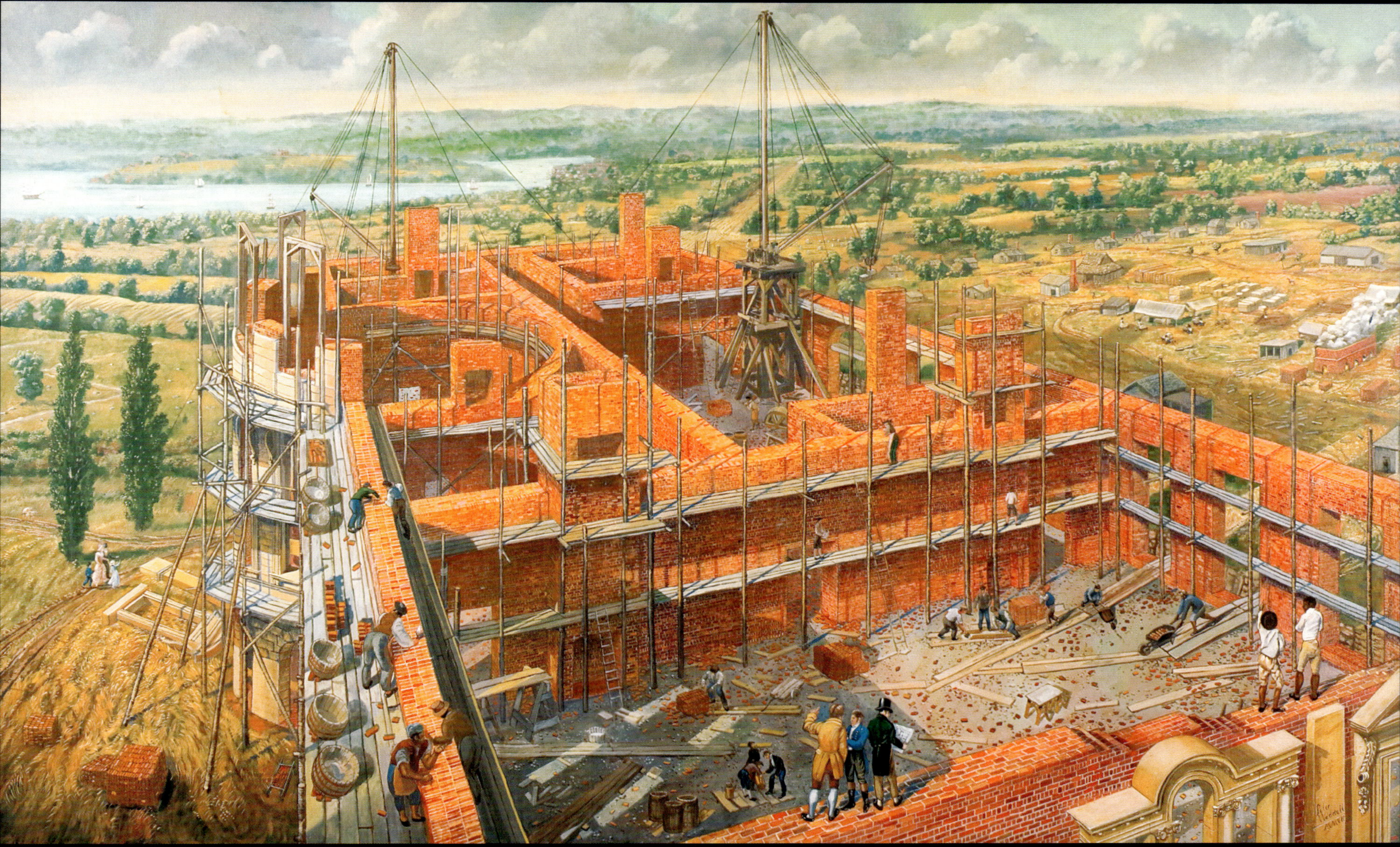

oil on canvas 49" x 72"

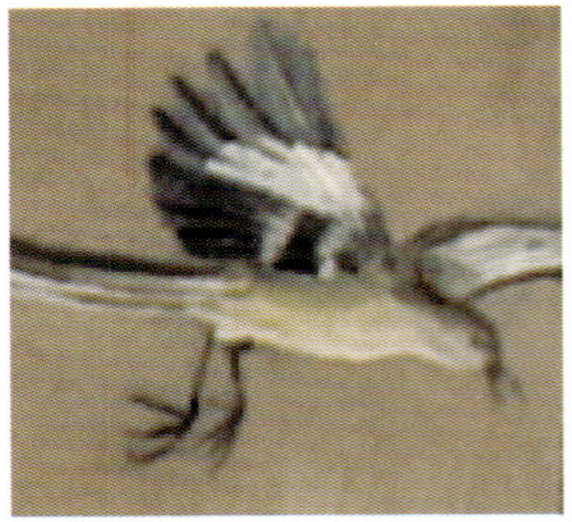

A Bird That Whistles

In Jefferson's Cabinet • 1803

PRESIDENT THOMAS JEFFERSON TOOK OFFICE ON THE THEN-INAUGURATION DAY OF MARCH 4, 1801, following a party win in the contentious campaign of the previous autumn, and the bitter congressional balloting that followed in January and February to determine between Jefferson and Aaron Burr, who would be the president and who the vice president.

From the beginning Jefferson had thought the President's House too grand, so when it became his home he cut it down to size in use. This room, a formal levee or reception room under Adams, Jefferson converted into his office. In re-creating it, the artist has selected from among Jefferson's actual furnishings. Beneath a lofty, eighteen-foot ceiling the president has left the polished floors bare and has scattered his interests over the room—maps, experimental potted plants in the windowsills, a surveyor's telescopic theodolite, and of course books. The bird that flies so familiarly about is a mocking bird befriended by Jefferson and taught to communicate by whistling.

Among Jefferson's prime interests for the nation was the unexplored west, most of which was not yet in American hands. We see him here in 1803, the year of the Louisiana Purchase, before news of that great event came in July. The rugged outdoorsman, Meriwether Lewis, who stands before him, was 28 years of age, at the White House ostensibly as his secretary but in fact there to study under the president for a secret expedition overland to the Pacific Ocean, perhaps to find the Northwest Passage by sea to Asia; but more to gain intelligence about the country. They met daily. At last, when the surprising news of the Louisiana Purchase reached the White House, Jefferson appeared on the front steps on the Fourth of July and announced the great achievement to a crowd celebrating the holiday outside. Lewis, meanwhile, left through a back door to join William Clark, but forgot his wallet. The setting you see here soon passed into history and the room became the State Dining Room, which it was when President John F. Kennedy, on October 1, 1962, greeted Nobel Prize winners he had assembled for dinner: "I think this is the most extraordinary collection of talent, of human knowledge, that has ever been gathered together at the White House, with the possible exception of when Thomas Jefferson dined alone."

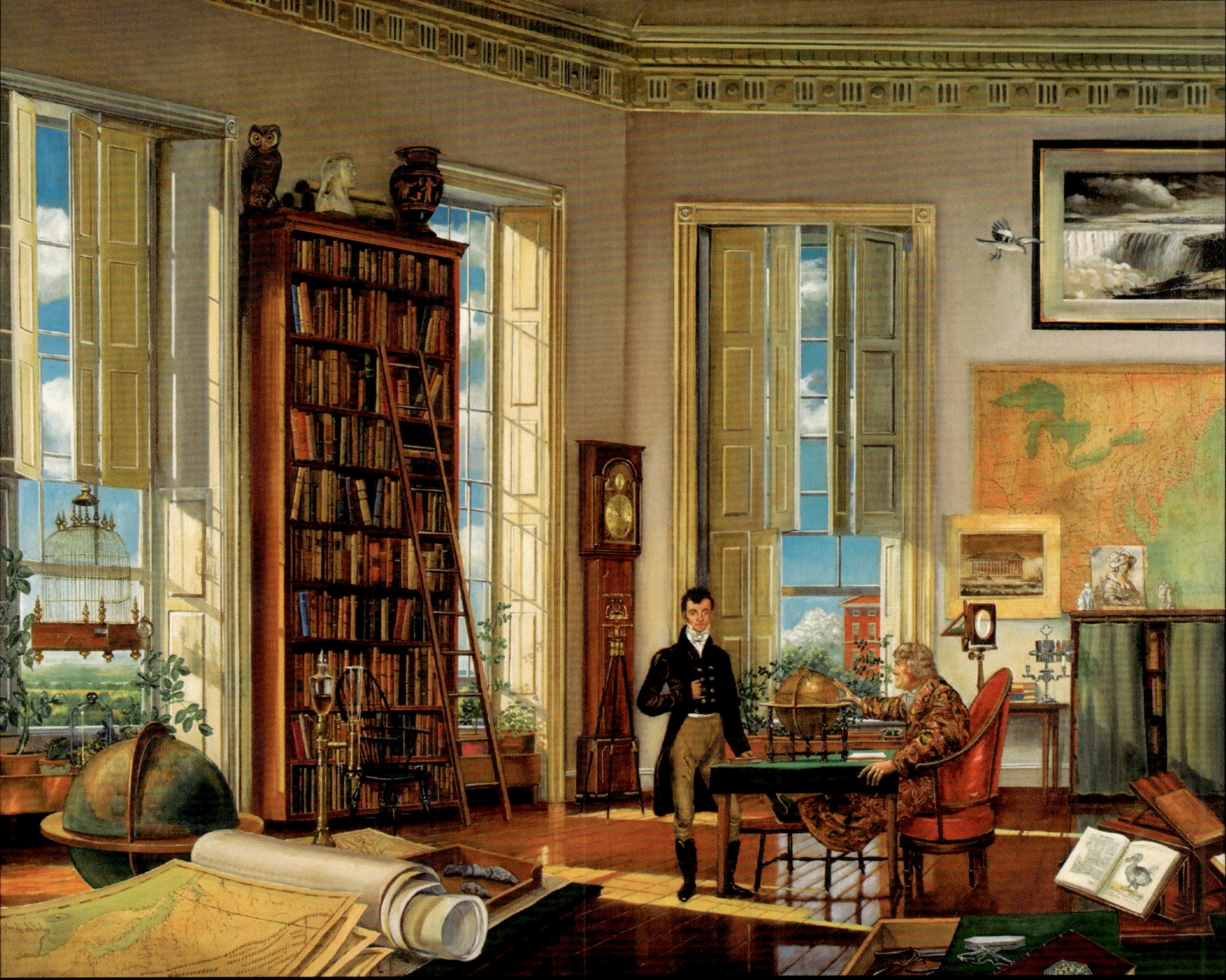

oil on canvas, 48.5" x 60.5"

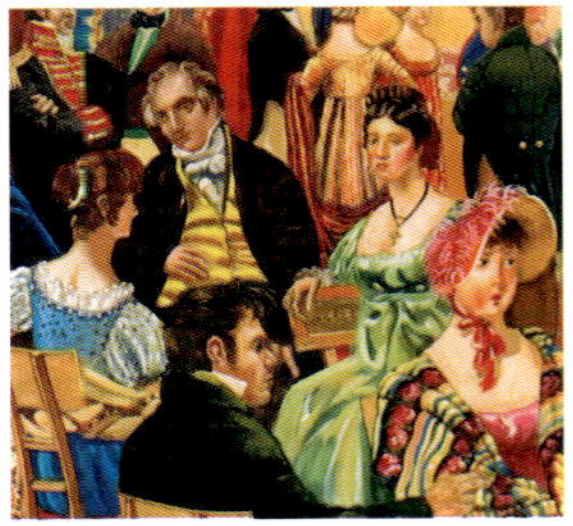

The Splendid Mrs. Madison

In the "Elliptical Saloon" • 1810–1814

THE MOST FAMOUS HOSTESS IN THE HISTORY OF THE WHITE HOUSE WAS DOLLEY MADISON, a lady in whom legend and fact intertwine now, as they often did in her own time. In this painting the artist shows the principal drawing room of the Madison White House—today's oval Blue Room—sometime during the years from 1810 to 1814, when her celebrated "drawing rooms" or salons were the apex of social life and private politics in Washington.

Elected as a man of action, the soft-spoken James Madison was a distinguished statesman, the principal author of the Constitution, former secretary of state and at last president of the United States. Some years of trouble with Britain had climaxed during his administration with America's declaration of war against England in 1812. Two relatively quiet years passed before Britain defeated Napoleon, and was free to turn her military energies to her former colonies. This she did without further delay.

One can imagine the tensions beneath the surface at this White House as the first months of 1814 passed by. The prime purpose of Mrs. Madison's weekly drawing room receptions was to create a forum, where in social association and conversation the two diverse political parties in the Congress might begin to pull together in the crisis. For the drawing rooms Dolley Madison extended matchless hospitality, mixing interesting local people with the often homesick lawmakers from out of town in a warm, elegant setting. She poured red wine and whiskey or rum punch in profusion; the iron stove in the kitchen below was fired up for ham, beef, turtle soup, and crab and the most delicate sweets.

The Madisons took their ideas for the drawing rooms to the White House immediately after his election and the outgoing Jefferson had to step aside for the architect B. Henry Latrobe and the curtain-maker Mary Sweeney. The result, ironically, was that the room reflected high fashion in London at the time in the latest "Grecian" taste, as did the women guests, in their filmy Grecian gowns. The room re-created here vanished in flames on the night of August 24, 1814, a casualty of the British invasion, to live again only now in oils on canvas.

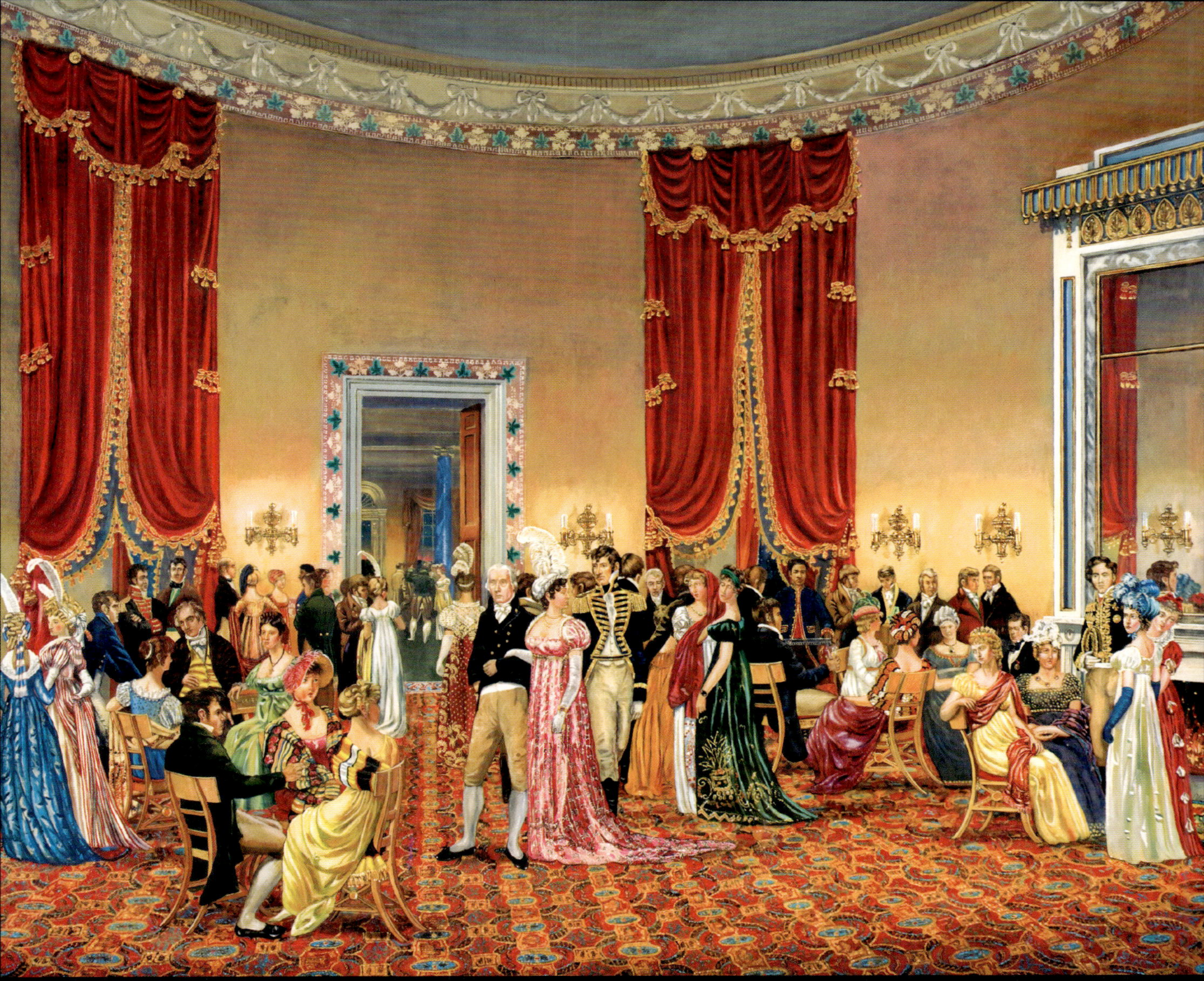

oil on canvas, 48.5" x 60.5"

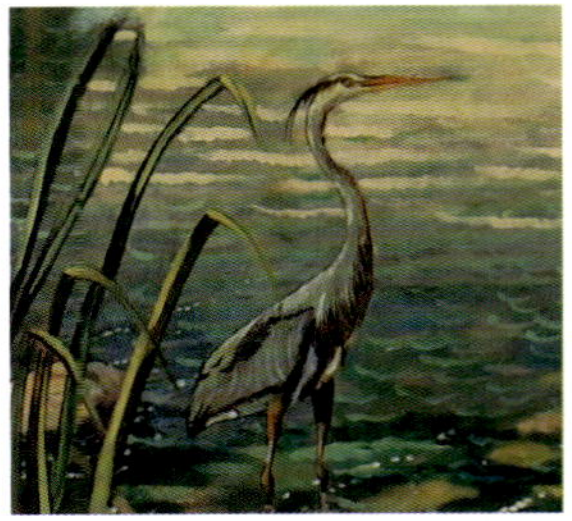

Tiber Creek: The Bathers

John Quincy Adams Takes a Deadly Chance • 1825

TIBER CREEK NOW FLOWS SAFELY BENEATH A MASONRY VAULT, over which passes Constitution Avenue. In the 1820s, the open creek raced dangerously to the Potomac River through the sweeping landscape you see here. From marshy creek banks the land rose gently to the elevation upon which the White House stood. Its muddy realities were covered by grasses and wild flowers.

President John Quincy Adams, sixth president of the United States, and son of the second president, liked to take his exercise swimming early mornings when the weather was welcoming. The fifty-seven year old president never swam alone, and his usual companion was the White House steward Antoine Michel Giusta. On June 13, 1825, his son John, who was in his early twenties and his father's secretary, also went along.

On the morning the picture represents, the president decided to commandeer an abandoned boat, row it down Tiber Creek across the river then swim back, keeping the boat nearby for safety. Suspicious that the boat was too leaky, young John stripped-down, and waded away to the river, intending to dive in and accompany the swimmers on their return. But by the time the boat was swept into the Potomac from the swift creek, it was filling with water; danger was quickened by a sudden squall from the north, and the boat began to sink. Giusta, already naked, jumped into the water. The president scrambled overboard, still dressed, and would have been weighted down by his clothes, had Giusta not been at hand to pull him to the shore.

The president lay gasping on the riverbank, attended by his son, while Giusta departed to secure a vehicle. A visitor passing by saw the whole thing and quickly reported it to the waking capital, where the subject of a president dying in office remained current for days afterward. The incident, widely reported, was naturally an embarrassment to the president. He described the near-tragedy in detail that evening in his diary, concluding: "By the mercy of God our lives were spared, and no injury befell our persons." And he pledged to try no further feats of athletic skill but to "strictly confine myself to purposes of health, exercise, and salutary labor."

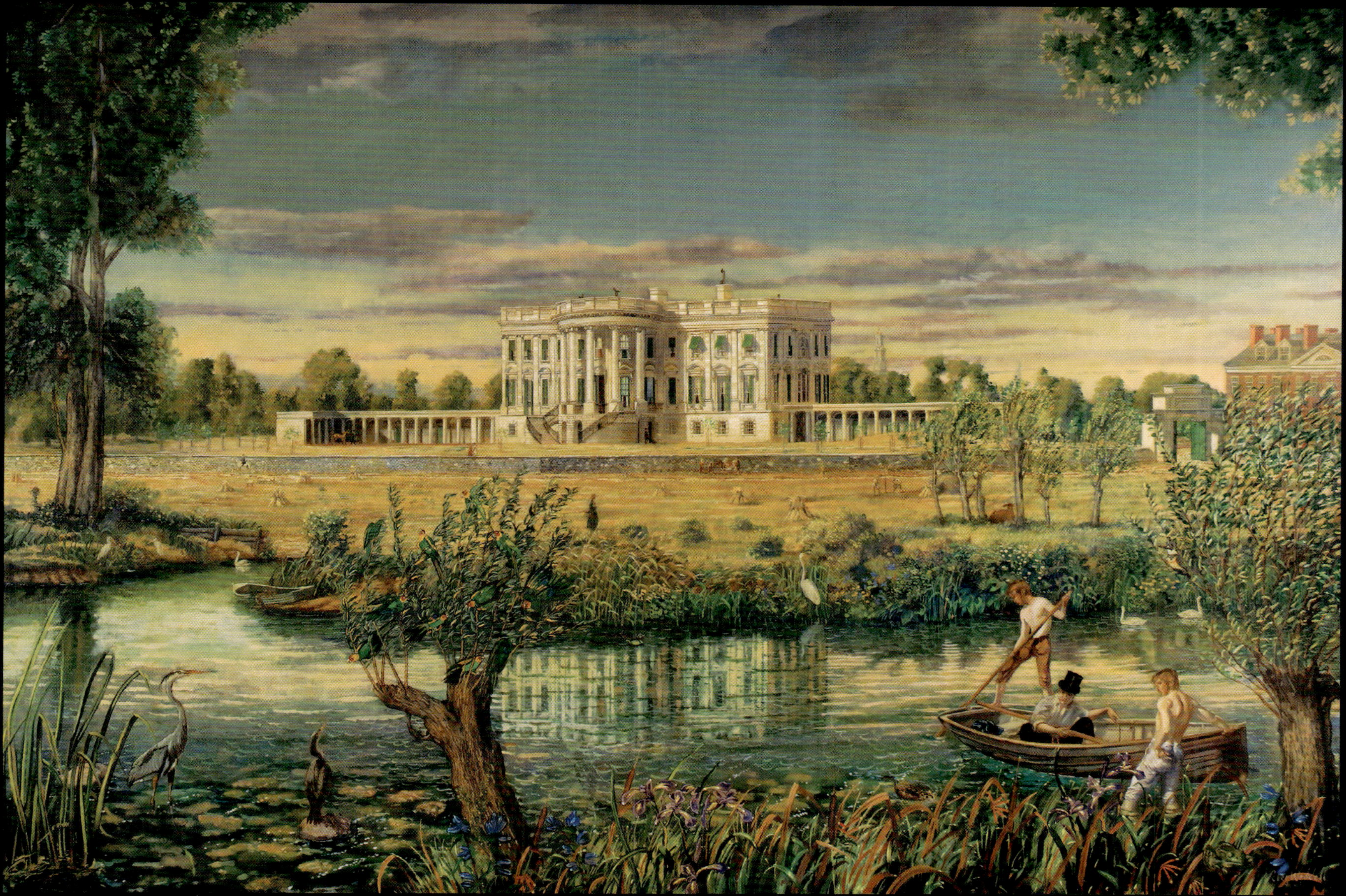

oil on canvas, 48" x 72.5"

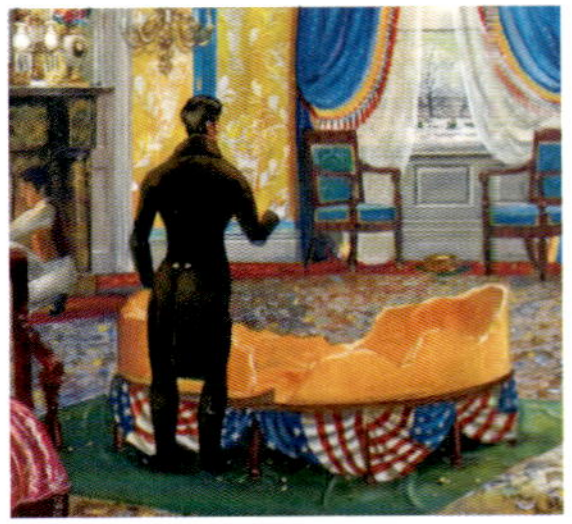

The Great Cheese

Jacksonian Democracy Enjoys a Special Treat • 1837

The East Room, the largest interior in the White House, was conceived in planning the house as an official gathering place where, among other ceremonies of state, Congress would convene to present bills to the president. President Jefferson disposed of state ceremony early-on, so there was no urgency to complete the room. It was unfinished when the British burned the house in August 1814 and although reconstructed by 1817, it remained without interior decoration until in 1828 when Congress appropriated the necessary funds to furnish it for the incoming president, Andrew Jackson.

Completed in 1829, during the first year of Jackson's administration, the East Room is shown here in about 1837, having served as Old Hickory's stage for his two terms. It was a rich ensemble of glass, mahogany, and silk; the walls were papered in lemon yellow, and twenty-two spittoons served the national habit of the time. Reception crowds, alerted by the Marine Band's marching strains, rushed to see Andrew Jackson enter through the tall arch to the left, and pause for a thrilling moment. Wrapped in his blue cape, the greatest American hero since Washington posed beneath the halo of gold stars and sun rays that his aides had pasted on the wallpaper above him.

The White House was first opened to the public in 1801 by Jefferson, and by Jackson's time the East Room was the main interior shown to visitors. The East Room's attractions increased notably late in Jackson's administration when the president received a thousand-pound cheese from New York admirers. Put first in the Entrance Hall for two years, the cheese gradually lost its better fragrance, so, stinking mightily, the by-now famous "Mammoth Cheese" was towed to the East Room where the visiting public was invited to cut off and eat as much as it pleased.

The artist captures the moment, re-creating in the opulent interior the human tone of a railroad waiting room. Foreigners looked upon such White House scenes patronizingly as negative expressions of American democracy. In spite of it, artist Waddell's visitors, dressed nicely—a requirement for admission—enjoy their free presidential cheese and pause to drink in the delight—as we might do today—of simply being there.

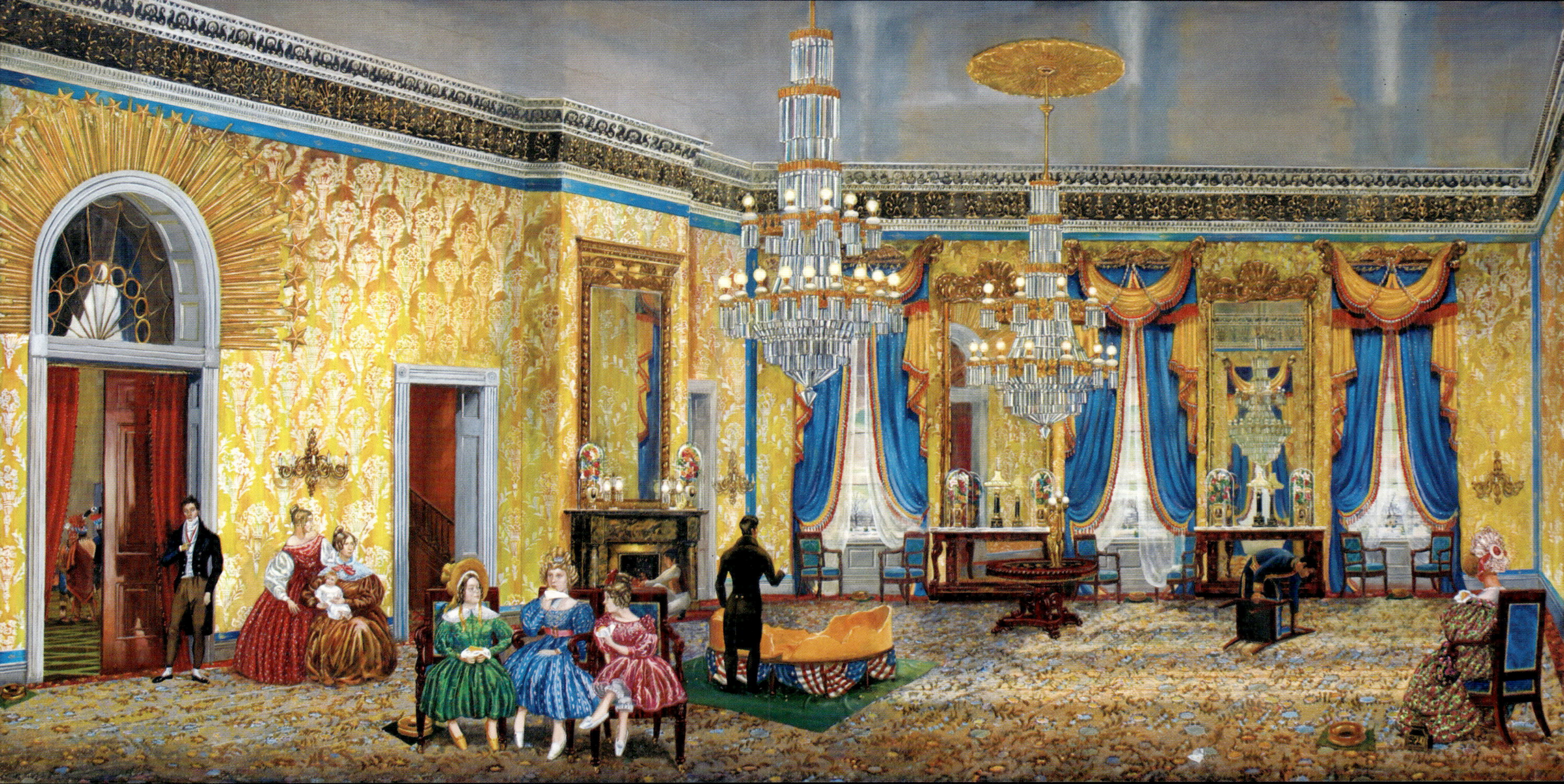

oil on canvas, 48.5" x 108.5"

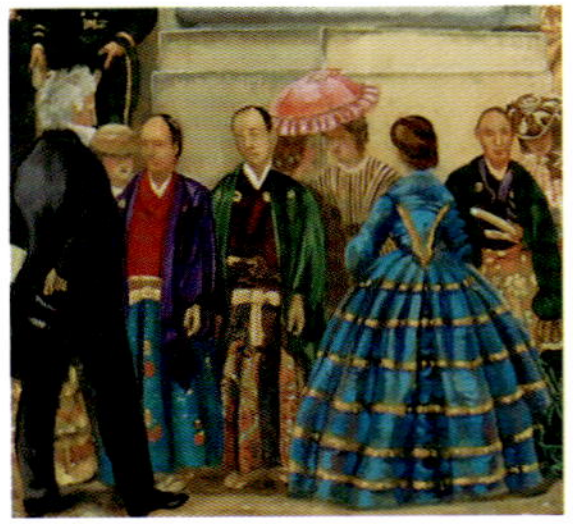

Visitors From the East

President Buchanan Greets Visitors from Far Away • 1860

Those who lived it remembered the 1850s as the most elegant era the White House had ever known. Emerged from the war with Mexico, its western boundary stretched to the Pacific Ocean, the United States was rich with promise, and while the decade was cursed by economic crisis in the Panic of 1857 and the violent debate over slavery, few would deny the social splendor of the decade at the White House.

The White House in the 1850s was central to the diplomatic community in Washington, just as it is today. Foreign countries began sending their representatives to the United States as soon as the nation was formed. Well-educated, refined and worldly, the diplomats, all male, were well funded by their native countries to live noticeably. They gave an international sheen to the workaday capital.

The artist takes us here to a spring evening in 1860 when the first representatives of Japan have come to call upon the president. Their visit was a response to the late Commodore Matthew Calbraith Perry's 1852–54 expedition to Japan and the resulting treaty that opened trade with the United States. Styled "ambassadors," the party consisted of three samurai and their entourage of seventy-four attendants. Some of the gifts they brought to the president remain in the White House today. Most of the other diplomats seen here carried as their official title "minister." Along with their wives, they arrived in fine carriages with the president's other guests, military leaders, luminaries from Congress, and prominent citizens. Surviving diaries, letters, and reports reveal that the Japanese visitors found the Americans disorganized, emotional, and too informal, quite unlike the Americans, who were fascinated by their guests and massed in crowds to see them.

Buchanan's White House was perfection itself. A hospitable, decorous man, Buchanan and his niece Harriet Lane greet the guests here with handshakes and welcoming words. In so elegant a setting, politics and passions were already paving the road to civil war. The last hours of antebellum America are captured in this tranquil twilight moment among the columns of the President's House.

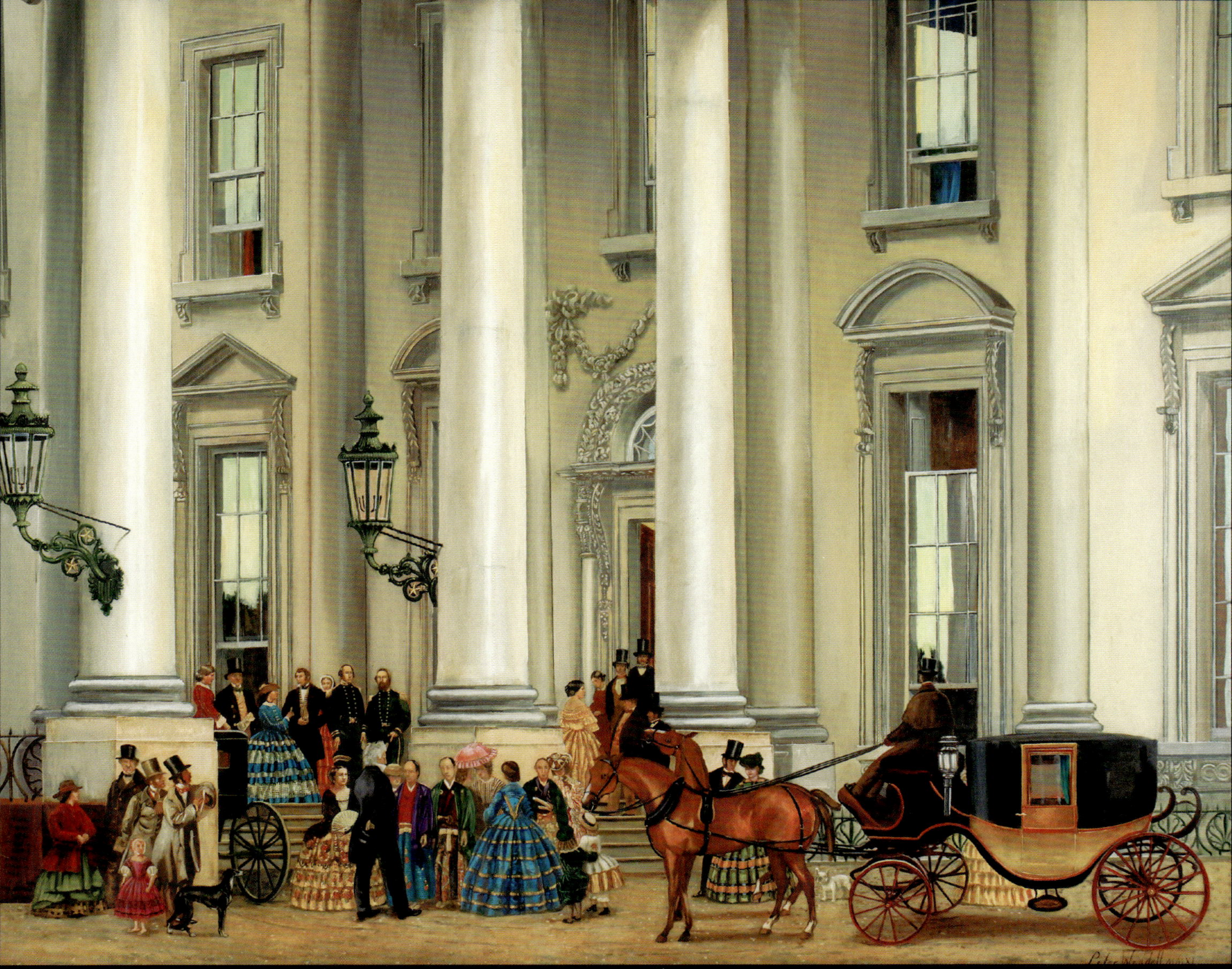

oil on canvas, 48.5" x 60.5"

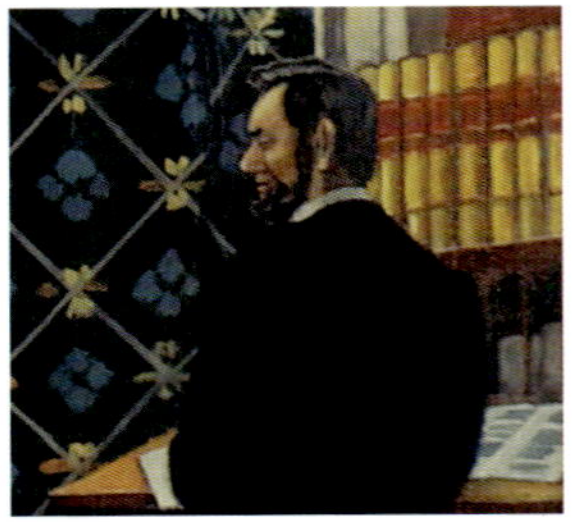

The Visit

A War Worker Calls for a Favor • Late 1862

ONE OF THE MOST REVERED HISTORIC INTERIORS OF THE WHITE HOUSE IS THE ONE THAT PRESIDENT LINCOLN OCCUPIED AS AN OFFICE. Located in the east end of the second floor, it shared the upstairs with the family's private living quarters. Although intended as a bedroom, it had been used for an office since 1817.

Historical documentation, written and visual, is fairly complete in recording what Lincoln's office was like, and meticulous research has guided the artist in creating this painting. Old photographs show the wallpaper pattern, if not the color; a contemporary drawing shows the furniture, wall maps, and other details, even the table lamp that uses a rubber hose to borrow gas from the chandelier above. The artist found in the records of the Library of Congress that at this time Lincoln had checked out Henry Wadsworth Longfellow's *Hiawatha*, Frank Forester's *Field Sports* and *Fish and Fishing*, and these are duly placed on a stool in the foreground.

On the long, plain wooden conference table, on New Year's Day 1863, Lincoln signed the Emancipation Proclamation, freeing the slaves in the Confederate states and revitalizing the purpose of the war.

The day represented is late in 1862; Lincoln has a visitor, an old acquaintance, Mary Livermore. She is a public-spirited activist, but more importantly to the president, a strong worker for his election in 1860 and a very effective fundraiser for the United States Sanitary Commission. The Commission's volunteer contribution to the well-being of the soldiers and military hospitals was monumental. She has come to solicit a handwritten draft of the Emancipation Proclamation to auction at a "Sanitary Fair" fundraiser in Chicago. She was later to report back that the pages of foolscap with Lincoln's handwriting brought $3,000, nearly one eighth of the president's annual salary of $25,000.

This room remained the office of the presidents of the United States until 1902. Twenty-seven years later President Herbert Hoover designated the room the "Lincoln Study," furnishing it with his collection of Lincoln books and pictures. When President Harry S. Truman rebuilt the White House from 1948 to 1952, he re-created the room as the Lincoln Bedroom, which it remains today.

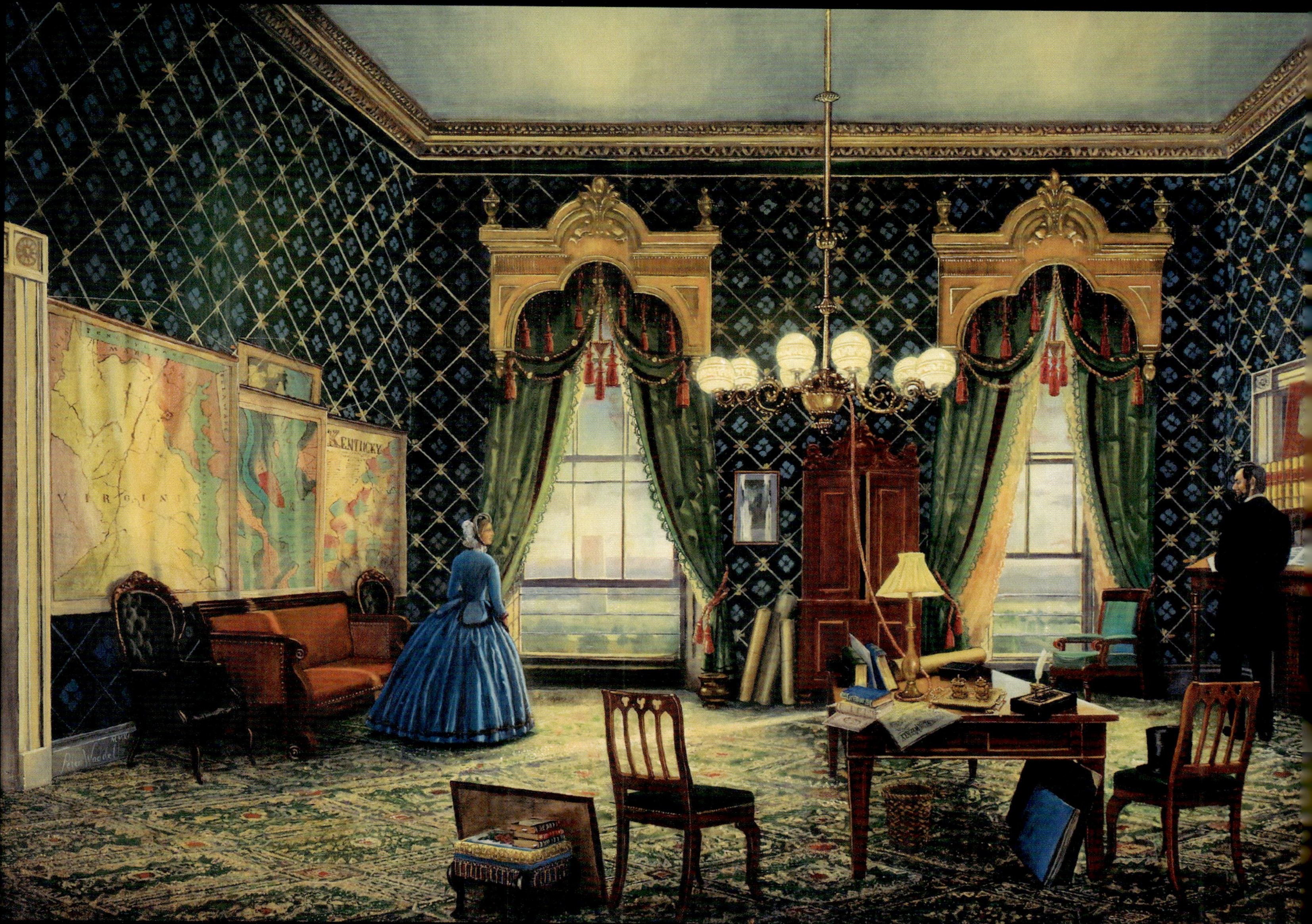

oil on canvas, 36.5" x 48.5"

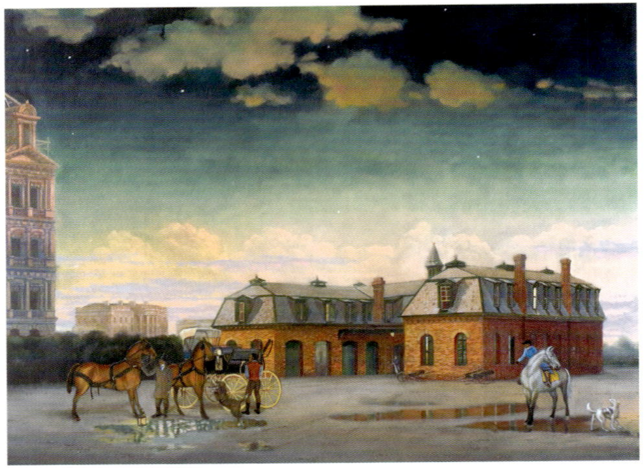

oil on canvas, 48.5" x 60.5"

A Favorable Day

The White House Stables on the Day of Grant's Second Inauguration • 1873

DAWN BREAKS OVER THE WHITE HOUSE STABLES ON MARCH 4, 1873. The grooms and coachmen are up early to prepare for President Ulysses S. Grant's second inaugural parade. Details have been taken by the artist from historic photographs. The carriage in the picture, which was a sporting vehicle made to accomodate hunting dogs, still exists.

This stable was the fourth built at the White House. Designed and built in 1871 by the government architect Alfred B. Mullett, it was ample in plan, the lower floor outfitted with twelve wooden stalls and stone-paved floor. The African American stable staff lived upstairs, where rooms were provided for the two grooms, Charlie Lee and Jerry Smith, and an apartment for the stable master, Albert Hawkins, who is represented at the left of the picture.

Jesse Grant, the president's youngest son, and Nellie, his only daughter, kept their ponies here and remembered the easy pace of the daily conversations their father had with Hawkins about horses. President Grant's favorite was the thoroughbred Cincinnati given to his care during the war by a dying man. The president found Butcher's Boy, later his famous harness horse, pulling a meat wagon; the butcher demanded and received the outrageous price of $600. Jeff Davis, with an easy gait, was captured by Union troops in Mississippi. Algonquin and the beloved Egypt were distinguished veterans of the general's Civil War battles.

Government vehicles assigned to the president were kept washed and polished in the stable and included the formal carriages, a barouche, a phaeton and an elegant landau, in which First Lady Julia Grant made her weekly social calls. A light market cart transported the children to public school, and a broad-gauge road wagon served on deep-rutted country roads. Extensively remodeled in 1890, the stable continued to be an integral part of White House life until its conversion to a automobile garage in 1909, and demolition two years later.

The Confidant

First Lady Lucy Hayes and Her Maid • 1879

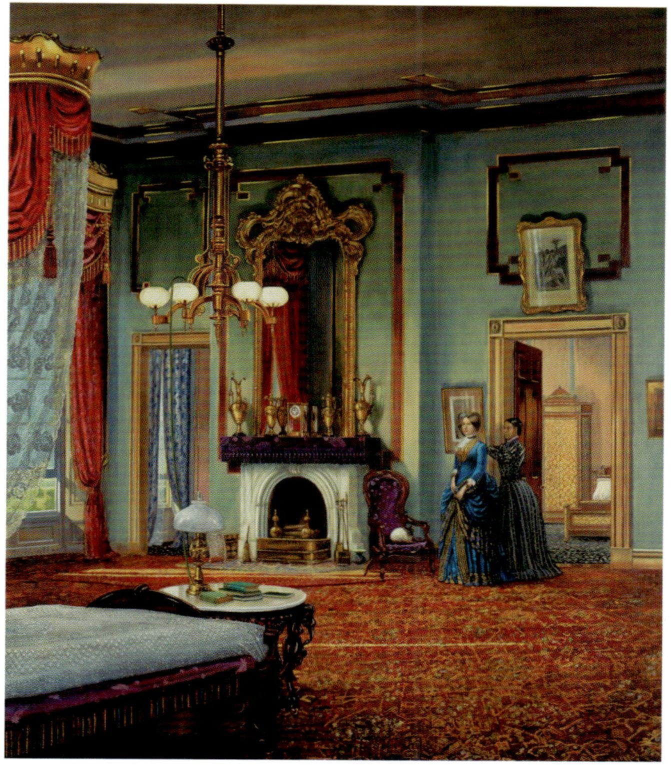

oil on canvas, 60.5" x 48.5"

PRESIDENT RUTHERFORD B. HAYES ANNOUNCED WHEN HE WAS ELECTED THAT HE WOULD SERVE FOR ONE TERM ONLY; this he did, and it was an uplifting four years for the country. With his wife Lucy, Hayes determined to return tranquility to a nation troubled by recent political scandal and economic depression. They set out to be a "model American family" in the White House. Recognizing value in the women's campaigns against saloons, Mrs. Hayes decreed a "dry" White House, banning alcohol from presidential functions. "Water flowed like wine," commented one diplomat after a dinner, but the American people admired the first lady's stand.

The artist visits a very private corner of the Hayes White House in this depiction of Mrs. Hayes and Mary Monroe. Standing in her bedroom, Mrs. Hayes is dressing for a formal reception. Mary Monroe, her maid from Ohio, is helping arrange the complicated silk afternoon dress. At the top of the grand staircase, just outside the room, Mary would stretch the first lady's 3-yard court-train for the dramatic descent to the company in the main floor below.

The fantastic rosewood bed with its gilded and draped crown had been purchased by Mrs. Lincoln nearly twenty years before (to President Lincoln's disgust), and the artist has sketched it where he found it today, in the Lincoln Bedroom. Through the open door can be seen the modern faux bamboo bedroom furniture Mrs. Hayes bought when she moved to the White House.

With their four children Rutherford and Lucy Hayes entertained more than any of the presidents before them. The events are forgotten, except for one, which they introduced in 1877—the annual Easter Egg Roll, still held at the White House.

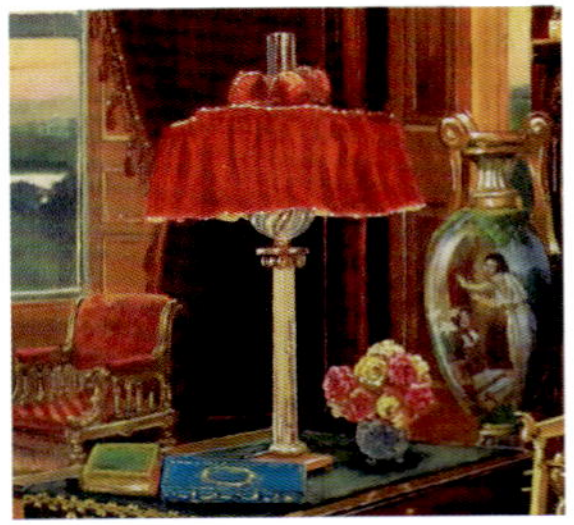

Composition in Red and Gold

A Comfortable Room Rendered Richly • 1883

The Red Room was the only complete interior Tiffany created for the White House. Redesigned in high Aesthetic taste (meaning "art-like") the room, was first called the Red Room some thirty-five years before, during the administration of James K. Polk. It is shown here about 1883, during the presidency of Chester A. Arthur, transformed from the old-fashioned room it had become. All the furniture was removed as well as the architectural elements; only the earlier gas chandelier remained. The marble mantelpiece was replaced by a new one of polished wood framing gilded Morocco panels, ornamental tiles, and brass. In the only surviving photograph that can be said beyond a doubt to be Tiffany's Red Room, the photographer placed his camera where the open door is shown here. Artist Waddell has selected a view nearly opposite, for which the photograph was supplemented by the contractors' written records.

Even as well-documented as the interior is, the historical record deprives the artist entirely of the original colors—which were indeed more color effects than single colors—but he has based his selections on the Aesthetic preferences of the time and the many written descriptions, which often stretch to describe the unusual tones and shades. Various types of glazing were applied to achieve dramatically nuanced color in the walls and trim, changing in the play of daylight through the tall windows and evening's light from the gas chandelier and kerosene lamp. As with the adjacent Blue Room, dark color at the base of the walls thinned as it rose toward the cornice, with applications of colored shellac. At the ceiling the Red Room was crowned by a galaxy of copper and silver stars that shimmered in reflection, contrasting with the absorbent walls.

Tiffany's were the first White House interiors that made news. Considered modern and artistic, the Red Room was probably the most highly acclaimed of all. A comfortable, even cozy room, it was still occasionally used as a family sitting room and often the place where the family received visitors. Here the long window is open to the South Portico, so that two of the president's three sisters, Molly McElroy and Malvina Haynesworth, might enjoy the good weather and the view. The Scottie beneath the table, named Tot, the favorite pet of Arthur's twelve-year-old daughter Nellie, gained a measure of newspaper fame by biting the president.

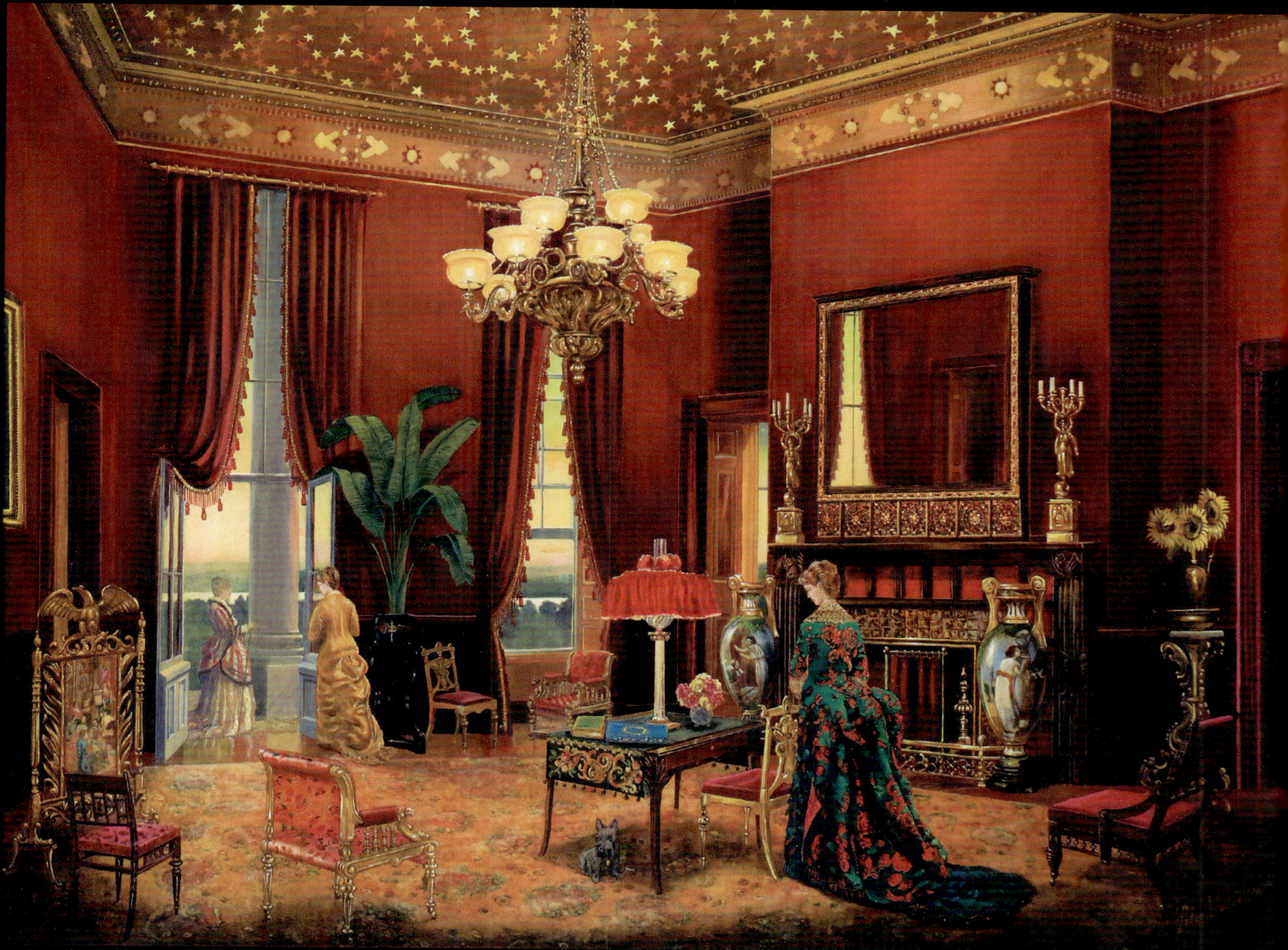

oil on canvas, 36.5" x 48.5"

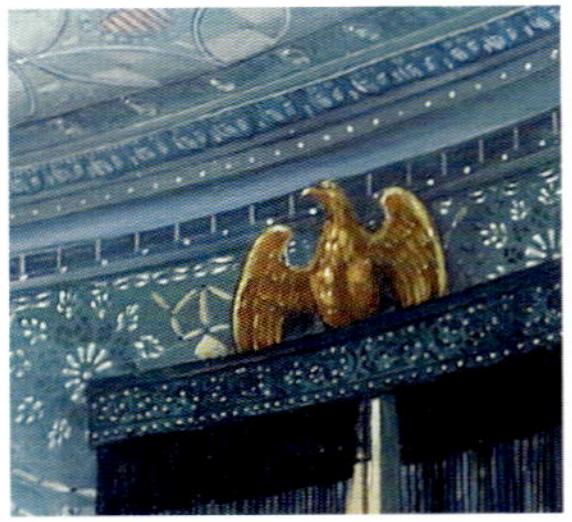

Something Blue

Captured by Color • 1886

THE MOST DISTINCTIVE OF THE STATE INTERIORS IN THE WHITE HOUSE IS THE BLUE ROOM. Located central in the plan, it projects toward the magnificent view of the Potomac valley. In planning a new office in 1909 President William Howard Taft elected to create an oval office, to replicate the shape and thus relate the official office to the historic White House.

Among the Blue Room's many guises in décor, perhaps the most ethereal was that created by Louis Comfort Tiffany in 1882 for President Chester A. Arthur, at the same time he built the colored glass screen in the hall immediately adjacent. Tiffany emptied the room of the old fringed and tufted decorations, and converted the historic oval space into a frosty dreamlike experience in blue, white, and silver. The artist here shows a contemplative Mrs. Grover Cleveland, at the age of 21 history's youngest first lady, who was married in the room in 1886, standing amid the Blue Room's dreamlike elegance.

The walls were a dark, absorbent blue at the wainscoting, and thinned with white and tinting to a reflective robin's egg blue toward the cornice. Overhead, snowflake and doily shapes in white and silver leaf covered the ceiling and fell to meet a storm of silver snowflakes. The room's colors form horizontal bands in shades of blue, a device carried out even in the curtains. An existing marble mantelpiece was reconfigured by the addition of glass tiles that reflected the firelight. White House antiques from the era of James Monroe are displayed on the mantelpiece. Silk canvas in two shades of blue covered the existing suite of furniture. The effect was one of being swallowed in a space in which architectural form and iridescent color unite as one.

Tiffany's decor was at the time four years old. Frances Folsom Cleveland is dressed for an evening reception. Her court train, measuring nine feet long from her shoulder, is as it will be arranged at her feet when she and the president stand in a receiving line. Faced with the facts of heavy use at the White House, Tiffany's nuances of color proved almost impossible to maintain, so practical considerations called for a less creative redecoration in 1890.

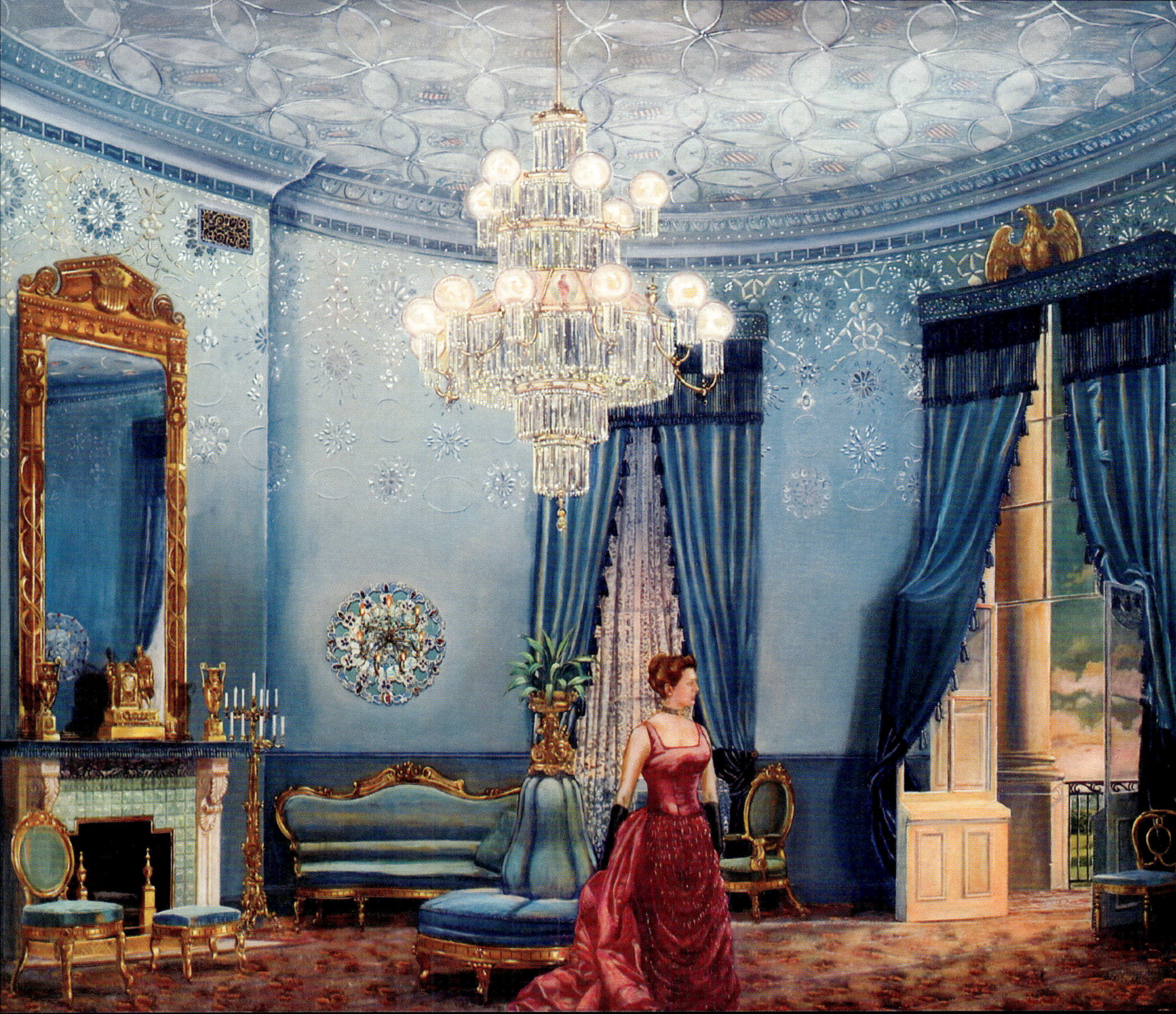

oil on canvas, 48.5" x 57.5"

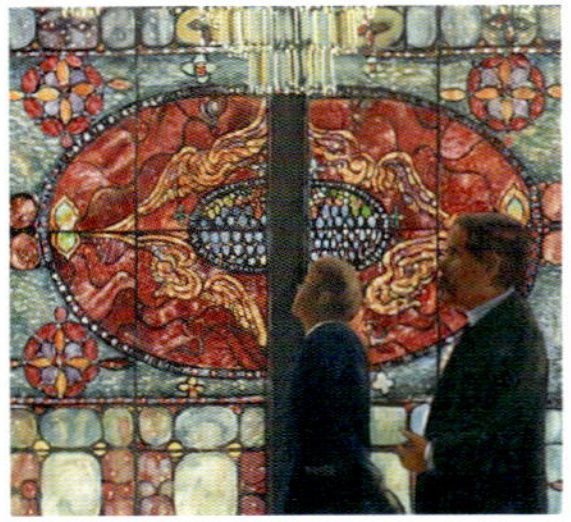

The Grand Illumination

Sunset of the Gaslight Age • 1891

PERHAPS THE MOST LEGENDARY OBJECT IN THE WHITE HOUSE PAST, apart from the Lincoln bed and Gilbert Stuart's portrait of George Washington, was removed a century ago and later destroyed. It was the "Tiffany screen" of colored glass that stood in the Entrance Hall a mere nineteen years, from 1883 until 1902. This popular expression of the Aesthetic taste in design was commissioned by President Chester A. Arthur from Louis Comfort Tiffany, the thirty-four year old artist then very current in New York art circles. It was a foremost symbol of Victorian taste.

Trained as a painter, Tiffany became interested in the relatively new opalescent glass, an innovative coloration created by introducing metal oxides to molten glass. With the White House as his showcase, he emerged from the project a famous man. President Arthur succeeded from vice president to president, following the assassination of James A. Garfield in 1881. He did not fit the hometown Garfield image at all, being a stylish widower from Manhattan. The new president celebrated the difference by turning to Tiffany to make the White House shine.

The glass screen was dazzling beyond all the rest of the Tiffany alterations. He replaced with opalescent glass the plain panes in an existing architectural screen that had crossed the hall since 1837 to block drafts. Peter Waddell found most details of the screen well-documented in the National Archives, but not the actual colors of the glass. In deciding the colors, he studied Tiffany glass, but in particular a window Tiffany had installed at Saint John's Church in Washington, D.C., in memory of Arthur's late wife Nell.

We visit the Entrance Hall in the year 1891, when President Benjamin Harrison converted lighting in the White House from gas to electricity. Ike Hoover, electrician, has switched a wall lamp, which erupts with harsh electric light. While the new light did not impact the screen excessively, in the rooms it negated Tiffany's effects, obliterating the iridescent paint colors. Unlike the painted surfaces, which were meant to reflect and absorb light, the screen's opalescent glass was made primarily to filter light, as it does here at the end of day, when the cold, early evening light from the north is warmed to deep, rich colors, as it passes through the screen.

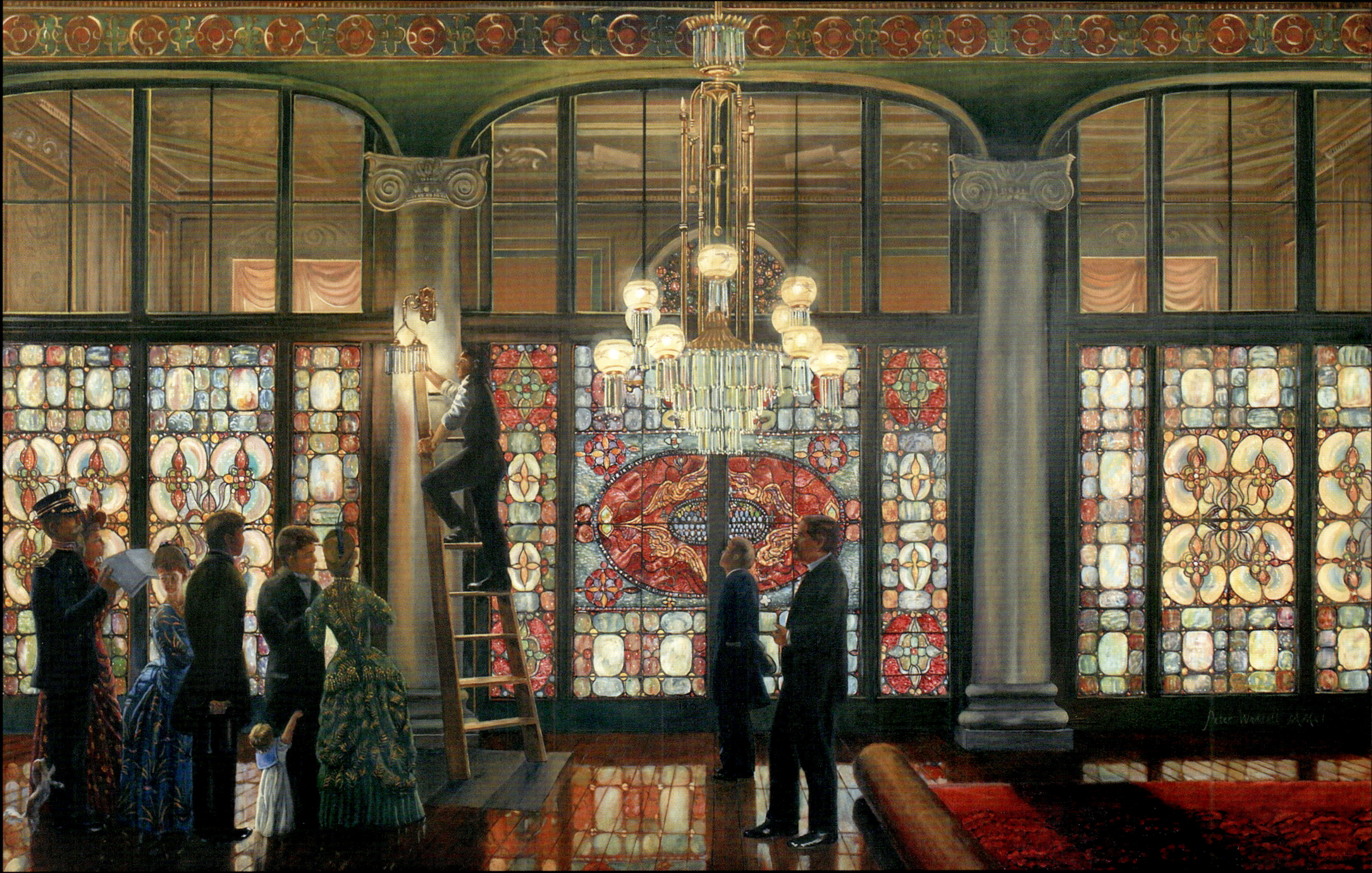

oil on canvas, 55'' x 73.5''

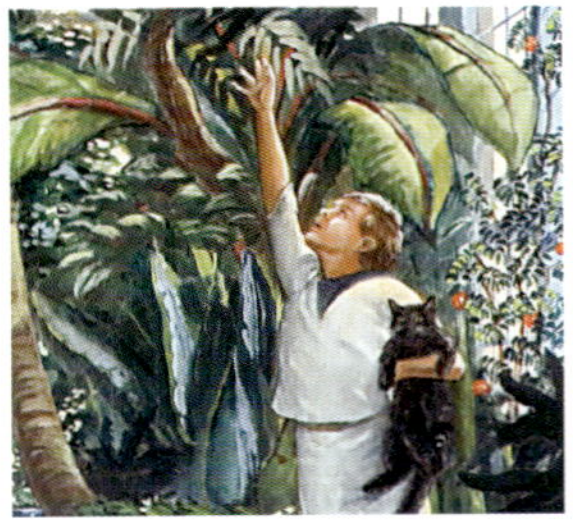

The Secret Garden

Last Days of an Exotic World Under Glass • 1902

THE ARTIST'S IMAGINATION HERE HAS BEEN SPARKED by both the photographs and extensive invoices listing hundreds of types of plants purchased for the White House greenhouse and conservatory. Andrew Jackson built the first greenhouse, an orangery, in 1833, which was moved to adjoin the house in 1856 and open off the west end of the main hall. After it burned in 1867 a more ambitious structure was built, then over the years expanded into a major greenhouse, with orchid rooms, cactus rooms, a rose garden, camellias in great number, seasonal flowers and the usual citrus trees. Closest to the house was the tropical room, seen here, filled with plants. Here Kermit Roosevelt, the president's son, plays with his macaw Eli Yale and his cat Tom Quartz, as his mother Edith Roosevelt looks on from the door into the White House.

No feature of the nineteenth-century White House was more popular with first families than this world under glass. Here the first family had privacy, sunshine, and the delight of plants and flowers. Paths, seemingly endless, led between avenues of low tables with terra cotta pots lined up on them, filled with plants. Flowers were cut to use in the house and send as bouquets to visitors in town. At the time of this scene, about 1902, four "bouquet makers" were on the White House staff and in their conservatory work room produced centerpieces, flower arrangements, corsages and floral offerings to be sent out with specially printed cards acknowledging the gift from the president and first lady.

The conservatory stood in various forms for about fifty years atop the West Wing or Terrace of the house. When in 1902 it was decided to remodel the White House, the architect Charles McKim with great difficulty convinced the Theodore Roosevelts that the "glass houses" should go, for they were an impediment to the historical authenticity of the original White House. At first the Roosevelts absolutely refused, cherishing the pleasures of the glass houses. But the symbolic importance of the White House to the nation, which only recently had been recognized a world power, won out. The conservatory, which was of metal, was disassembled and for a time reassembled in part on the National Mall. Today parts of it are incorporated into greenhouses maintained by the National Park Service in Maryland.

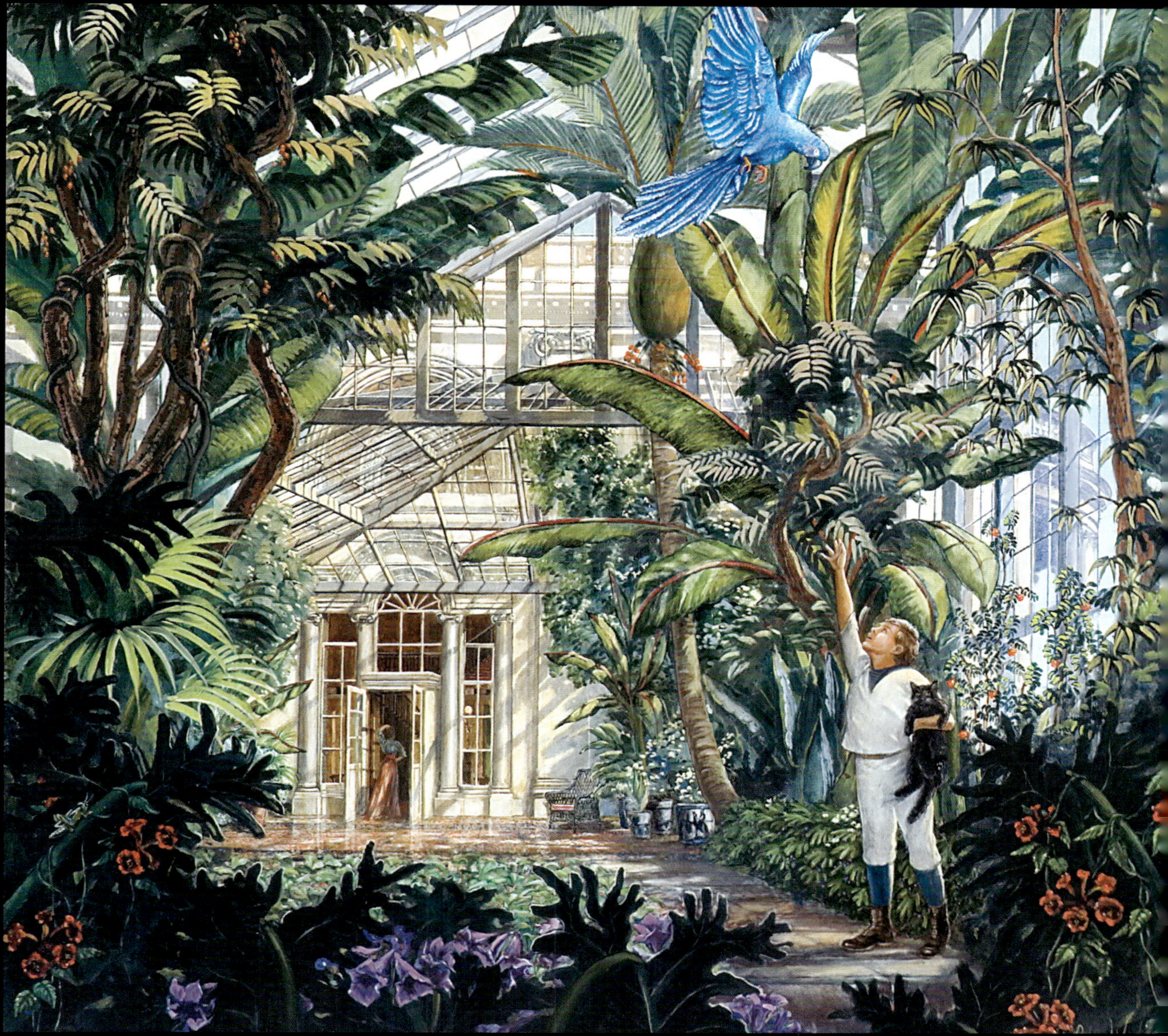

oil on canvas, 40.5" x 30.5"

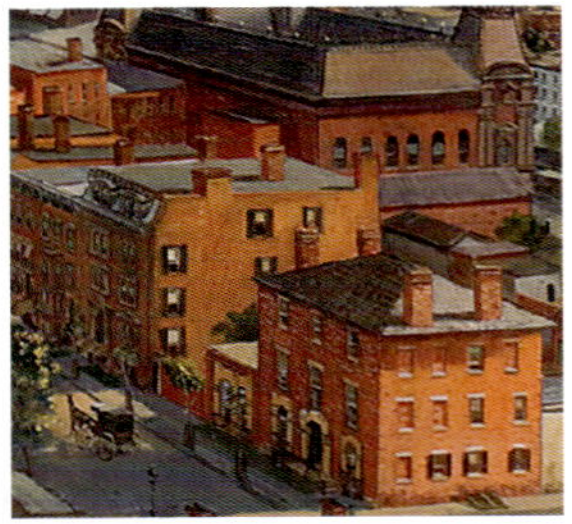

Lafayette Square

Once the White House Overlooked a Residential Neighborhood • 1902

PETER WADDELL'S PAINTING RE-CREATES THE HISTORIC SQUARE NORTH OF THE WHITE HOUSE IN 1902, the year Theodore Roosevelt remodeled the house. To the right of the White House, one can see that the conservatories have nearly all been removed from the roof of Jefferson's west terrace. At the end of this terrace the Temporary Executive Office is under construction. It would become the West Wing. Construction on the east or left side of the house has begun to replace the east terrace, demolished 1869. This will become the new social entrance. At that time the area around Lafayette Square was still residential, so the White House still projected the large scale that had set it apart for a century.

The artist has placed you well above the rooftops, higher than any place to which you could have climbed. Sixteenth Street, immediately below you, is part of an axis in the city plan that pierces the White House and intersects a similar axis from the Capitol on the Mall beyond it. At the intersection Major L'Enfant, planner of the city, envisioned a monument to George Washington, but when the Washington Monument was finally built, it was moved, as you see here, to avoid the original site's marshy ground.

Lafayette Park, which the square surrounds, was commissioned by President James Monroe in the early 1820s, and named in honor of General Lafayette during his visit to America in 1824 and 1825. Andrew Jackson's statue on his rearing horse Sam Patch became the centerpiece of the park in 1853, an American masterpiece in bronze. Of interest along the Square are steepled Saint John's Church at the bottom of the picture, and to the left, the house on the corner was where the widowed Dolley Madison lived for the last thirteen years of her life. Directly across the Square from Mrs. Madison's house is the historic Commodore Stephen Decatur House, built in 1819 and rich in history, now home of the National Center for White House History, under the auspices of the White House Historical Association.

After many years of alteration and demolition, the low-scale residential quality of Lafayette Square has been restored, thanks to the vision of President and Mrs. John F. Kennedy. Once again it is possible to sense the original scale and setting of the White House in a tranquil context of old houses, heroic monuments, big trees, and the Park's winding paths and carpet lawns.

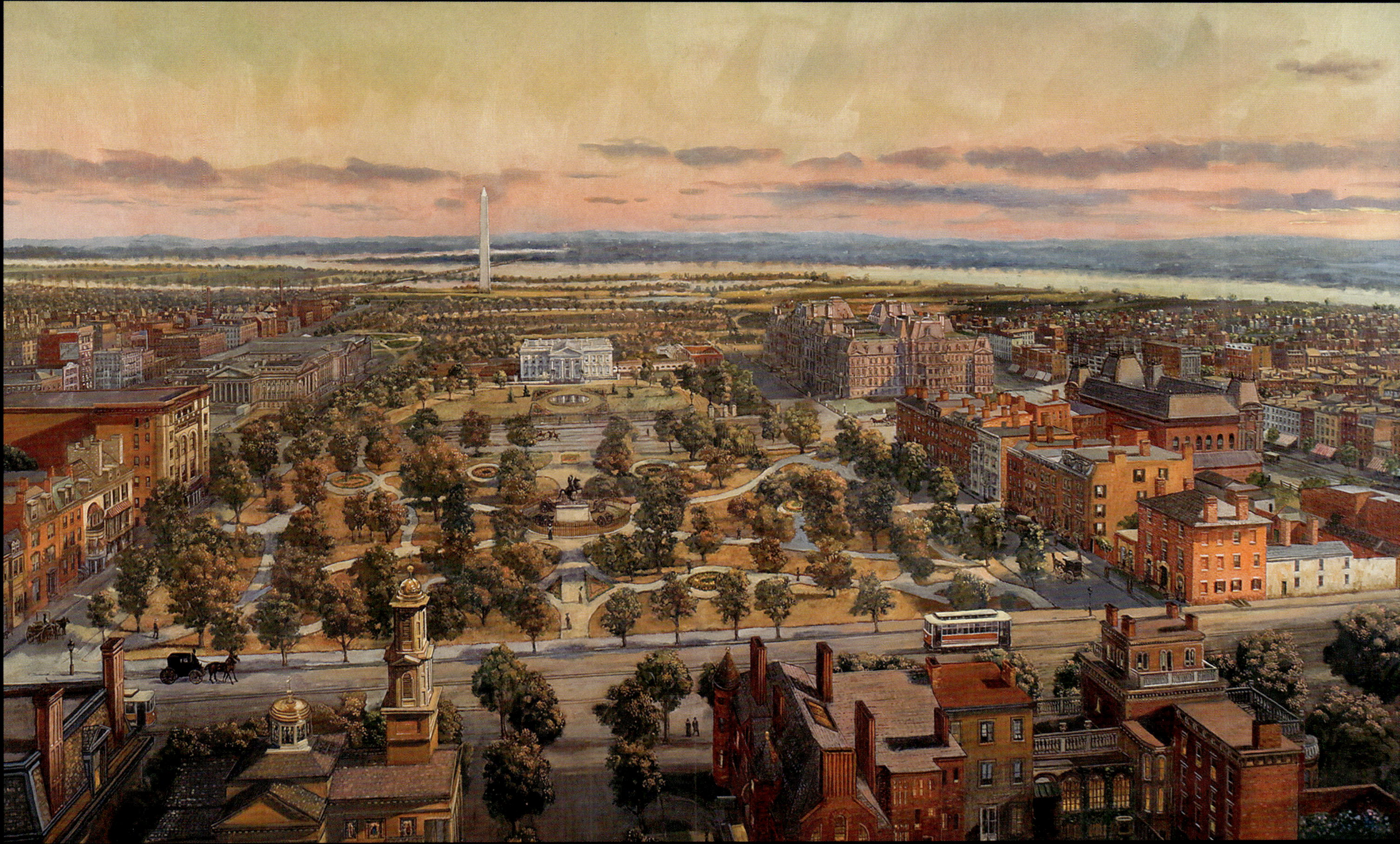

oil on canvas, 48.5" x 60.5"

About the Artist, Peter Waddell

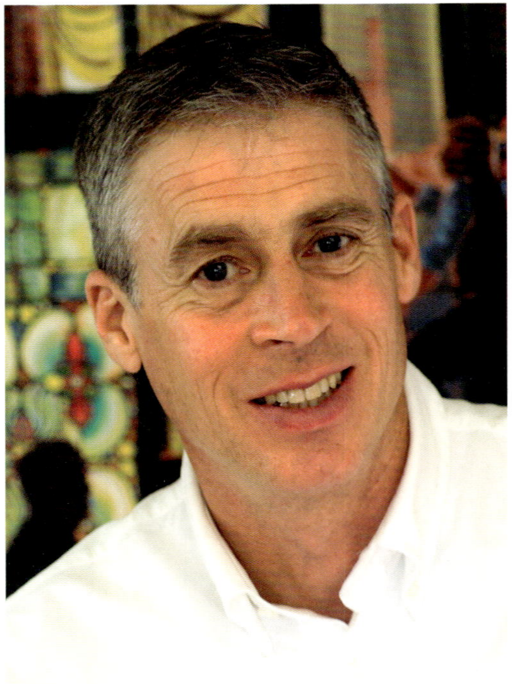

Best known for his paintings of Washington, D.C., history and architecture, Peter Waddell has previously created works about the Capitol in the nineteenth century (*Inside the Temple of Liberty*); the role of Freemasons in the creation of the Federal City (*The Initiated Eye)*; the history of the Octagon; and numerous other commissions for historic sites including Mount Vernon and Tudor Place. Recent smaller works can be found on the streets of the city around the National Cathedral, and in the Kalorama neighborhood where Peter has been involved in the Call Box Project, placing historical images on former police and fire call boxes. His contributions to the arts in Washington, D.C., were recognized in 2010 when he received the Mayor's Art Award.

Peter Waddell was born in Hastings on the East Coast of New Zealand in 1955. A child of vivid imagination, his ability to paint and draw was always encouraged by his parents Colin and Penny. From Colin, owner of a cabinet making firm and former soldier in Egypt and Italy, he gained his love of craftsmanship and fascination with the ancient world; from Penny, a theatrical costumer and librarian, his ability to create dazzling effects. After considerable success in New Zealand as an artist, Peter came to Washington in 1992 to learn the secrets of the masters as a copyist at the National Gallery. Enamored with America and its history from the start, Peter became a United States citizen in 2002. Peter is artist in residence at Tudor Place in Georgetown.